STEFANIE MARVIN-MILLER

Salvo

This book was professionally typeset on Reedsy.
Find out more at reedsy.com

For Joshua — who saw the broken pieces of me and stayed.

For James — whose laughter stitched light into the places I thought would never heal.

For Willow — who showed me what joy looks like when it finally learns to trust again.

And for Leland — my steadfast shadow, my healer, my proof that love can save a life.

For every survivor who still wakes up fighting:
your story is not over.
You are your own salvo — the return fire, the rise, the reason the darkness does not win.

Contents

Preface

There are moments in life that split us in two — the person we were before, and the person we are after. *Salvo* was born in the space between those two selves.

For a long time, silence felt like survival. In the military, silence was expected — demanded — when I was assaulted not once, but twice by fellow service members. Speaking out brought retaliation. Speaking out cost me pieces of myself I didn't know I could lose. But it also led me here — to reclaiming my story, to rediscovering love, to finding the strength I thought had died in that silence.

This memoir is not just about trauma. It's about what happens *after*. It's about the small salvations in life — a dog who became my service companion and my healer, a husband who stood beside me when I couldn't stand on my own, and a journey that led me from surviving to living.

Salvo means "a sudden burst" — of gunfire, of noise, of energy. For me, it's the burst of truth breaking through years of suppression. It's the shot fired toward reclaiming power, voice, and hope.

I share these pages for every survivor who has ever wondered if their story mattered, if they were believed, or if healing was possible. You are not alone.

This is my salvo.

And now, it's yours too.

— *Stefanie Marvin-Miller*

Introduction

I've been told more than once that I shouldn't be here. That I shouldn't have survived the storms life has thrown my way. Maybe they're right. But I'm here anyway—breathing, standing, and telling my story.

Before I wore a military uniform, I was a child of chaos. My childhood was a battlefield of its own—marked by a peripheral father figure, punctuated by hurtful hands, and haunted by secrets no child should carry.

I learned to wear armor long before I ever put on a uniform. I learned to keep my secrets hidden, to swallow my shame whole, to press on even when the weight of survival felt too heavy to carry.

I thought the military would offer me a fresh start—a chance to prove myself, to forge a new identity out of discipline and courage. In those early days, I believed the uniform would protect me, that the camaraderie of my brothers and sisters would be a shield. But even in the rigid order of the barracks, my ghosts found me.

The first time it happened, I was stunned into silence. A fellow soldier, someone I trusted, stripped me of more than just my body—he took my sense of safety, my dignity. I was left with questions that haunted me in the darkness: Why me? Why didn't I fight harder?

I tried to bury it, to keep moving forward. But the weight of that betrayal pressed on me like a second skin. I told myself it was an isolated incident, a crack in the armor. But the second time it happened, I understood that the war I was fighting wasn't just on the battlefield—it was in every barracks, every formation, every time I closed my eyes and saw his face.

The shame was suffocating. I tried to tell someone, but the system was built to keep me silent. The words felt dangerous, like they would only make things worse. So I carried them in my heart, a wound no one could see but me.

There were nights when the weight of those memories crushed me. Nights when I held a bottle of pills in my hand, convinced the only way out was down. The night I finally swallowed them was the night I decided I was too tired to keep fighting.

But fate had other plans. My attempt at oblivion was interrupted by a friend who refused to let me go. I woke up in a hospital bed, tubes in my arms and a heart still beating. It was there, in that sterile room, that I realized I had a choice: to let those wounds define me, or to fight for the life I still had.

That choice led me to a new mission—one I never expected. I was introduced to the idea of a service dog, a partner who could stand watch over the nightmares I couldn't shake. I remember the first time I laid eyes on him—big, soulful eyes that seemed to understand every secret I carried. He wasn't just a dog. He was a guardian, a living, breathing reminder that healing was possible.

He learned to interrupt my panic attacks, to nudge me back to the present when the memories threatened to drag me under. He slept beside me when I was too afraid to close my eyes. He taught me that vulnerability didn't have to mean weakness—that I could still be strong, even in my moments of fear.

This memoir is the story of a soldier who has lived through a thousand battles, most of them invisible. It's a story of scars—some etched in skin, others buried so deep they only surface in nightmares. It's a story of betrayal, of trauma, and of the long, hard road back to trust.

But it's also a story of redemption. Of how love found me when I thought I was unworthy. Of how a four-legged angel gave me back my sense of purpose and the courage to keep moving forward.

This is my story, unflinching and raw. A testament to the human spirit's refusal to stay down, no matter how many times it's knocked to the ground. A promise to anyone still fighting in the dark: you are not alone. There is hope. There is healing. And there is life beyond the battle.

Chapter 1

Grand Haven, Michigan, was a town that seemed to have been painted by the hand of God in a palette of blues and greens. Tucked along the shores of Lake Michigan, it was the kind of place that wore its seasons like a well-loved coat: the bitter cold of winter giving way to the gentle thaw of spring, the golden warmth of summer evenings, and the crisp crackle of autumn leaves underfoot. I grew up in that town of unsalted-sweet air and lighthouse towers, and though my life was anything but tranquil, the town itself stood as a comforting backdrop, always there, always unchanged.

The streets of Grand Haven were lined with trees that arched overhead, forming a green tunnel in the summer. In winter, those same branches turned into a web of frost and icicles, sparkling in the pale sun. The downtown area was where everyone gathered—at the farmers market on Saturday mornings, at the Coast Guard Festival in August, at the musical fountain light shows that danced every summer night. It was a town where faces were familiar, even if you didn't know their names. Everyone had a place, even if they didn't know how to claim it.

My childhood, though, was a different sort of story. The lake was a constant presence, lapping at the shore with an unending rhythm, but inside our small, weathered house on Mercury Drive, chaos reigned.

My parents' marriage was a battlefield, the kind of place where silence could be just as sharp as any spoken word. My mother learned early how to tiptoe around the edges of that tension, how to read the shift in the air when a storm was brewing. The gentle lilt of the Lake Michigan waves seemed to mock the turmoil within our home.

Yet even as I carried the weight of those years—of fear and confusion and the bitter taste of disappointment—Grand Haven was the balm I didn't know I needed. The lighthouse at the end of the pier became a symbol to me: its steadfast beam cutting through the fog, a promise of light no matter how thick the darkness. I would sit there sometimes, toes buried in the cold sand, and watch the waves crash against the rocks, feeling like they understood my silent storms.

The people of Grand Haven were a kind of family, too—one that didn't know about the battles inside our home, but one that offered smiles in passing, warm greetings in the aisles of Meijer, and casseroles when someone's grief was too much to bear alone. It was a town of shared stories, of whispered prayers, of small kindnesses that felt like lifelines.

Looking back, I realize that my story wasn't just one of survival. It was about finding solace in the constancy of a place, in the laughter of neighbors, and the gentle hush of a lakeside breeze. It was about learning to see beauty in the everyday, even when the world inside my home was anything but.

Grand Haven was more than a setting; it was a lifeline. And this is where my story begins.

I was Stefanie to most everybody in the town, but I was so much more. I was PFC Stefanie Marvin, Stef when my parents were angry, Peanut to my Grandma Marvin, I was Stefanie Marvin, later, Stefanie Marvin-Miller, Noodle, to my husband. StefanieAnneMarvin. StefanieAnne. Stefanie. It had been whispered, hissed, yelled, spoken, and crooned. I was a daughter, a sister, a stepchild, a friend, and a soldier.

I grew up with public school teachers for parents, and a non-denominational Christian. I'd lived in six different houses, three states, and four cities by the time I turned thirteen. I loved the Grateful Dead, Paul Simon, and tie-dye, and had best friends named Lauren and John Roscoe.

Eighteen and pregnant, my mother married my father. Three months later, he knocked her around their living room. She left or fought back. Left and came back. She wouldn't always instigate arguments, but she did. He bruised her eyes, her cheek bones, he broke dishes. He sold drugs and did acid in broad daylight, while I had marijuana seeds sticking to my arms, but he didn't break her. By the time she became pregnant with my little brother, Harrison, she'd finally found the strength to leave him for good. With the help of her twelve-year-old brother, Brandon, she packed what she could before my father came home. For Harrison's safety, he was later adopted into another family—a choice made out of love and desperation.

We were alone, with my mother, my uncle, and me in the front seat, driving away as quickly as we could.

By the time my stepfather came into the picture, Mom and I had already built a patchwork life in our little town of Grand Haven, living in a few different places with front yards that she and I would spread a blanket on, waiting for the "pizza dude" to come deliver our food. Mom had one job, then another. She was a waitress at our local dive, called

Rendezvous, and taught me how to read during the downtime on her shift, on the back of the paper place mats that they would use. One evening, a man saw Mom and me sounding out words, and paid for our meal. My mom never forgot that moment, even though I can't remember anything other than the chocolate milk they would serve in red plastic cups.

She worked as a nanny for our local chiropractor, and watched his two children, Lauren, and John. John was seven days younger than I was, Lauren was two years older than us. My mother took us to parks, to paint, or to get corn dogs from our town boardwalk. I remember the sun and hearing rollerblades on the boards from that time. That was my favorite job that she worked, it gave me my two, life-long, best friends, more like siblings, really.

LaurenStefanieJohn, LaurenieSteffieJohnny.

She'd yell those names, or speak them with love, always together, rarely ever separate. We'd play together, and we would get into trouble together, even with different fathers, I was never seen as different from them. Horseback riding lessons included me, there on the same days, riding the same horses, doing the same chores, right alongside them. I remember Nick, the huge, brown, gentle horse that let me reach a canter.

My mother loved the three of us, and showed as much affection to Lauren and John as she did me. Some of the best days were when she would put on her purple overalls, covered in sunflowers, tie her long, brown hair back with a bandana, open all of the windows, and blast "Cheeseburger in Paradise" by Jimmy Buffett, or "Scenes from an Italian Restaurant" by Billy Joel, with each of us playing an air instrument.

Mine was the piano, always the piano. I remember the smell of pine sol, and the cool breeze from Lake Michigan coming through the windows.

My mother was optimistic, artistic, and imaginative, except for the rare occasion when she would lose her cool at us, and scream the names LaurenStefJohn. That's when you knew you had stepped in it. She was kind, generous, and full of life. She'd have friends over, or have a friend live in the spare room that we had in one or two of our apartments. My mother loved helping, and giving whatever she could.

When she reconnected with Michael, a high school acquaintance, she didn't think it would work, because years prior, he refused to let her drive his father's car, because she didn't have a driver's license, ever the Boy Scout. She had a child, she'd already been divorced by the age of twenty-three, but they fell in love anyway. I was enamored by him, anyway, even though she tried to keep us as separated as possible. He was twenty-five when I met him, and when he married my mother, and promised to be a father, but to also never get in the way of my real father; a noble, steadfast, boy scout, who brought over a stereo system, and knew how to cook good, belly filling food. He never forced the issue of me keeping my last name of Marvin. He never asked me to call him "Dad" or "Father". His own parents were more excited to get a granddaughter than anything. They never batted an eyelash at the fact that I came from a different father, or that I was still very close to my father's family. They just loved without limits. We left our small apartment on Clovernook, and moved into a duplex in Spring Lake, a town over, where there was a big front yard, and a small half acre of trees in the back. I got my own room, and even got a canopy bed-the dream for a five year old girl.

My new little sister came home to that duplex, named Madeline, after

Michael's mother, who had passed away when he was nineteen years old. Madeline, Maddie, Maddie-Baddie. She was my little sister, my charge from the very beginning. It was a very serious job, and one that I took to heart.

From Spring Lake, we moved back to Grand Haven, into a brand-new, top-of-the-line trailer home. If you had asked me, as a six-year-old girl, I would have told you it was the coolest thing in the world to get my own bathroom, to have a tree, with branches low enough to climb, and trees covering the empty lots next to us. This was the dream. We were a little family, there, living out in the woods of West Michigan.

We moved and moved. My stepfather, a teacher, couldn't find work anywhere. The economy was going down by that point, like a sinking ship. Our life raft was the city of New Orleans, Louisiana, clear across the country. Michael had put out resumes everywhere, hoping for anything, while holding down a job at a Burger King, bringing home chocolate chip cookies every other night.

Once we reached New Orleans, crossing Lake Pontchartrain by way of an enormous bridge that seemed to stretch on forever, the horizon shifted before our eyes. The city appeared like a mirage—huge and dark, with a rain cloud hanging low over its skyline, hammering it with thick drops of warm rain. The air itself felt alive—humid, electric, and heavy with something I couldn't yet name. It was as if the city was breathing, pulsing with its own rhythm, one that neither of us from Grand Haven could yet understand.

Culture shock doesn't even begin to describe what we felt stepping into that world. New Orleans wasn't just another city—it was a living organism. It sang from every corner: jazz spilling out of open windows, the faint scent of gumbo and cigarettes in the air, laughter rising up from porches and courtyards. The sidewalks were cracked but beautiful, the oak trees hung heavy with Spanish moss, and time itself seemed to slow down, moving to the lazy cadence of a saxophone somewhere in the distance. Our small-town innocence dissolved almost immediately. Life in New Orleans was louder, bolder, freer—and unapologetically itself. It didn't care who you were before you arrived; it demanded you adapt, or be left behind.

Two years passed in that strange, magical city, and it began to shape us in ways we didn't yet realize. But in August of 2005, the air grew different. Still. Heavy. The kind of stillness that comes before something big enough to change everything. Hurricane Katrina loomed on the horizon like an unspoken fear, whispering warnings that grew louder each day. We watched the news, we heard the predictions, but none of it seemed real—not until it was.

When the storm finally came, it was a monster. It swallowed New Orleans whole. The wind screamed through the streets, the water rose faster than anyone could imagine, and the city we had grown to love— the music, the color, the chaos—was drowned beneath a gray, endless sea. Thousands lost their homes. Thousands more lost their lives. It wasn't just a storm; it was a reckoning. It tore through everything we thought was safe.

By some miracle, we had left the day before it hit—fleeing inland, unsure of where we were headed, only that we had to keep moving. When the rain began to fade behind us, I remember looking out the back window and watching New Orleans disappear, swallowed by distance and water. We didn't know then that we would never go back.

We drove through the night, the hum of the tires a kind of lullaby. I fell asleep somewhere in the blurred darkness of Louisiana, lulled by exhaustion and fear, and when I woke, the world had changed. The humid, storm-soaked city was gone. Outside my window stretched green fields and white fences, horses grazing lazily in the morning mist. Murfreesboro, Tennessee—a place I had never been, but one that would become the next chapter. The city that had once taught me how to live had been replaced by quiet land that would, in time, teach me how to begin again.

We lived in our uncle's house for 3 months before we moved into our new house, our first house, which we owned. It had a backyard, a garage, and an upstairs with rooms for both my sister and me. It was like a dream. I remember eating rotisserie chicken at our new table and singing at the top of my lungs in the living room.

I grew up through my teen years angry and confused, a storm of emotion that no one—including me—could quite contain. My father had moved to Tennessee, saying he wanted to be closer to me. I wanted to believe that, to believe I was worth the move, but something in me never fully trusted it. I didn't know what to do with that doubt, so I turned it inward and outward all at once.

I started sleeping with anyone who asked, as if each encounter could fill the void that no one could name. There was the cook from the Waffle House I met the day before, his hands smelling faintly of grease and cigarettes, his kindness mistaken for connection. I was chasing something I couldn't define—love, belonging, proof that I mattered— and it never lasted longer than the moment itself.

I blasted Grateful Dead CDs in my beat-up car, the windows down, hair tangled in the wind, pretending I was free while barreling toward every kind of trouble I could find. I smoked too much, drank when I could, and went looking for answers in all the wrong people and places. I was reckless, wild, and painfully alive, clinging to chaos because it felt like movement, like maybe if I just kept going, I'd eventually end up somewhere that made sense.

I don't know how my parents survived those years—how they managed to keep me in one piece when I seemed determined to shatter. But somehow, they did.

At eighteen, I packed up what little I had and moved out before I even graduated high school. I thought maybe living with my dad would be different, that maybe I could start over, find some version of the family we never quite got right. He tried—God, he really did—but fatherhood wasn't his gig. He meant well, but meaning well doesn't make you stay.

We parted ways quietly, the kind of silence that says everything. On the first day of my college classes, I came home to find a "For Rent" sign staked in the front yard of his apartment. That was how I found out he'd left. I stood there for a long time, books in hand, heart heavy but not surprised. It was just another lesson in how easily people can disappear—even the ones who promised they wouldn't.

I moved into the college dorms with a borrowed comforter and the kind of hope that feels rehearsed. The hallways smelled like cheap detergent and burnt popcorn, and the walls were plastered with posters for student events—things like "Movie Night" and "Pizza with the Dean." Everyone around me seemed so *normal*, so untouched. They talked about weekend plans and hometown boyfriends, and worked ten hours a week for pocket change, not survival. They laughed easily, the kind of laughter that doesn't hide anything behind it.

I'd lie in my narrow dorm bed at night listening to their music and muffled conversations through the walls, wondering what it must feel like to live without the constant hum of worry in your chest. To belong somewhere. To not always be waiting for the next collapse. It made me feel defective, like there was some invisible fracture line running through me that everyone else could see. Like I was missing the part that knew how to be ordinary.

By the middle of my sophomore year, the weight of that difference became unbearable. I drifted through classes, unable to care about grades or majors or what came next. I was restless in a way that sleep couldn't fix. I remember walking past the recruiters' tables set up in the student union—each branch with their crisp uniforms and glossy brochures promising adventure, belonging, purpose. They looked so certain of who they were, and I wanted that certainty like oxygen.

So I stopped. I walked up to one of them, a stranger in a perfectly pressed uniform, and I said the words before I could think twice. It wasn't courage—it was surrender. I forgot about college classes, about the smiling kids with normal families, about my mom and my dad and everything that felt too heavy to carry anymore.

And then, just like that, I raised my right hand and took an oath. It felt like erasing myself on purpose—like burning down the old version of me in hopes that something stronger might rise from the ashes.

Chapter 2

There were so many decisions, good and poor, that led to my decision to enlist in the military. There was the hole left by my father's absence, indifference, and addiction to acid and alcohol. There were my own poor life choices in men, in friends, in my college grades. My life was going in a direction that I no longer wanted to just accept. I thought I was hitting my rock bottom, and it was time to walk myself back to the woman that almost everyone in my life knew I could be.

To say that my decision to enlist was rash is an understatement to say the least. There were so many nights where I would drive as fast as my blue '65 Ford Mustang would allow me to go, where I'd feel more alive than I ever had been. Then, there were the days that I was so low that nothing, not even hunger or thirst, would motivate me to get out of bed. I thought the military would be my salvation—a way to prove I was stronger than the darkness, that I could stand tall in a world that kept trying to bury me.

I received nothing but support for my choice to enlist, no questions, no anger- just support and congratulations. I think everyone in my life, myself included, knew I didn't have many choices left on the path in life that I had set myself upon. I'd like to explain how well thought-out my decision to join the Army was, but it was a choice of convenience and the fact that there was an Army recruiter on my college campus.

As I left my parents on the sidewalk and was driven to the joint base where I would be processed into the military, we left each other with the understanding that who I had become up to that point was something that I wouldn't survive, and that enlisting was my last chance.

The night before I was driven to my basic training location, I stood in front of the hotel mirror, staring at my tired eyes and my scowl, tracing every freckle on my skin, as if to say goodbye to my old self.

Upon arriving at my basic training, simple instructions were given on everything- how to stand, sit, speak, look, and think. My brain turned on autopilot, and I spoke only when given permission to speak, moved only when commanded to march, and didn't dare touch my food until given the release command. No one here knew my history, nor did they care. The Drill Sergeants' only goal in my training was to make me a good soldier.

So, that was who I became, a good soldier. As I learned how to be a good soldier, I learned very simple truths.

While ruck marching, I learned that even though I was carrying an impossible weight on my back, I could bear it. I learned that even though I had made shitty choices in life, that I could atone and make better choices moving forward. While qualifying with our rifles, I learned how to be accountable for someone else's life and safety, and to never point a rifle at something unless you're willing to fire. On the obstacle courses, I learned how to work alongside people, and that looking back to make sure everyone makes it through is what makes or breaks your mission.

The military didn't just put me on autopilot and give my mind a chance to rest, it gave me a sense of belonging. It gave me a sense of duty and responsibility to myself and my brothers and sisters in arms.

I chose the job of Human Resources intently. The day before I made my decision, I called my dad, who was somehow sober and lucid, and asked him what military occupation I should sign up for. I was excited and determined to be in the first combat position open to women in the state of Tennessee. My dad, in a moment of clarity, calmly said, "Don't go for the combat role, just because it's open to women and you want to blow things up. Go for Human Resources, it will give you a job when you get out of the military."

That was one of the few times he was able to pull himself together and make an eloquent statement.

I was always told that people come into your life for a reason. At the time, I thought Drill Sergeant Ortiz was only in my life to cause me anguish, to punish us for one soldier's failing in our platoon. His lectures on safety and survival as soldiers went right over my exhausted head as my eyes struggled to stay open, and my arms trembled from doing push-ups right before said lectures.

He pushed us to better than our own personal limits, he taught us that there were no straight lines in nature, and that if you are going to point your rifle at someone or something, you'd better be damned sure you were going to open fire. It wasn't until our graduation that I fully understood him.

The roar of Graduation Day from basic training eventually subsided enough for me to find him in the sea of faces. DS Ortiz, a man who loathed these crowded, noisy affairs, was there. I suspected his aversion was twofold: a dislike for the spectacle, and perhaps, a quiet sorrow in releasing the soldiers he'd shaped. I asked Mom to commemorate the moment with a picture. When I said my goodbyes and expressed my gratitude, his declaration was powerful: "I would follow you into battle, soldier."

That would be the last time that we saw each other.

It wouldn't be until years later, after everything happened in the military, that we would reconnect over social media. He was so happy for me, for being in the place in my life that I was at the time, and for being a good soldier, just like he taught us. A few years after that chance digital encounter, I would later learn that he had passed away. When I read the words on my screen, the only thing that I could do was dig out that old picture of us together- me, gleaming in my dress blues, my smile beaming, and him, scowling and painting the somber portrait of a respected Drill Sergeant.

I still look back fondly on my experiences and memories of my initial training phases in the military. I would never understand how I was lonelier in my real civilian life than I was while serving. Finding myself in the military was like finding God; it was a higher calling to something bigger than myself and my own problems. It was a phase in my becoming, and I will never regret joining. It was what I needed to walk through to get to where I am today.

Upon my return home and after joining my first unit, I walked into the building with a sense of pride and a readiness to prove myself. Little did I know and fail to anticipate what I would experience while wearing that uniform.

Chapter 3

In 2016, I had been serving in my unit for 3 years. I was 22 years old, and I had the goal to be Sergeant Marvin before my contract ended.

In January of that year, I signed up to go on an extra mission to another Air Force base to deliver supplies. Being in Human Resources, I didn't really do much with transportation or logistics, so this was my chance to do so. I put on my uniform, the morning that we left, packed my rucksack with my belongings, and reported to my unit. I remember getting pulled over by a police officer for speeding that morning. Luckily, he took pity on me and let me off with a quick warning.

I knew a few people going on the mission with me, some well, some not at all. Our vehicles were loaded up, and it was time to get the Hell out of dodge and on the road. I was excited, as pathetic as that sounds, to be on a mission, to break from my normal military duties of paperwork.

The drive was beautiful, albeit frosty from the winter's cold, it chilled me to the bone in the metal cockpit of our vehicle. We saw the sun come up over the mountains and paint the sky in a burst of colors. It made me giddy just to witness it, and to find the beautiful in the mundane. As we pulled into the Air Force base and offloaded our supplies, we found our bunks for the night. I don't remember falling asleep as soon as my head hit the pillow, but I do remember waking up with a start of excitement.

As we exited the barracks and made our way towards the vehicles, with sleep still in our eyes, the sun was just starting to rise. I looked around, and in my breathlessness, I noticed just how high up in the mountains we really were. It was like God himself put the base there, just to give the service members a gift. The sun crested over a mountain top, then another, and then another, until the entire airfield was awash in colors of gold and orange. In my excitement, I managed to snap a picture before rushing to prepare to load up in the vehicles and come back home.

As I returned to my tiny apartment, I said hello to my cats and busied myself with unloading my gear, putting each item back to its proper place. A knock at the door caught me by surprise, I was still in my ACU t-shirt and pants. Besides throwing some pasta together for dinner, I hadn't even had a chance to take my hair out of its uniform bun.

I opened the door quickly as I realized it was Seth on my doorstep. I invited him in, with no inclination or suspicion of danger. What happened next would be burned into my brain and veins forever.

He came in and sat down on my old futon without invitation. I wasn't sure why he was there, I asked if he was ok, and I asked if he needed anything. He simply sat back and said, "I wanted to see you."

"I wanted to see you and see what's under that uniform."

As a woman, military or not, there are certain phrases, instances of body language, or smells of danger that will send a woman into fight or flight mode. This was one of them.

My muscles stiffened, and the hair on the back of my neck stood up on end. I inched my way towards my front door, slowly, with sweat dripping down my sides. In a matter of seconds, he was up, and I ran to my door, reaching for the doorknob. His arm was around my neck before I could let out a single strangled cry. I felt myself being pulled back into my bedroom, the only other room in my apartment.

Before I could register it, I was thrown onto my mattress. I reached for something, anything that I could use as a weapon. I found nothing except my mattress on the floor. A kick landed in my ribs, then another, and another, knocking every ounce of air out of my lungs. His hands were everywhere, on my body, on my clothes, grabbing my bun, lifting me up until his other hand was gripping my neck.

CRACK.

My head hit the pine wood wall panelling, not once, not twice, but three times. I could feel it, all of it. Each throb and ache as I started to drift in and out. My legs slowly stopped kicking, even though I was making promises to God to get me out of here, my legs just wouldn't work.

Then, darkness came over me.

I don't know how long had passed, but I woke with my head aching so much that I felt it in my jaw and teeth. I heard his pants buckle jingling in the silence, I was on my stomach, my ACU pants were torn and hanging off my leg like an old, worn-out flag.

I felt sharp pain, where he entered me, so sharp that it burned. My head was still pounding, and all I could do was let out the most pathetic, animalistic noise I could possibly make, feeling it come out of my chest and rise up in my throat.

He still didn't stop.

When he was finally finished, he was gone in what felt like seconds. I heard the door slam shut, and only then did the tears come flowing.

I could barely move. I could feel my lip swelling, my thighs burned from scratches, and bruises were starting to form. My ribs felt like they had shattered, and I could feel warm liquid drying in my hair. I rolled into my side, then slowly, ever so slowly, found my way up onto my feet. The world buckled and swayed in my vision as my feet hit the floor, and my legs, while shaking, held the weight of me upright.

I almost fell out of consciousness twice, but I made it to my tiny bathroom, illuminated by buzzing fluorescent lights. My right eye was red, and there was blood caked in my hair. I had ripped fingernails, and my whole body trembled, from fear, from pain, from everything. I tasted blood in my mouth and spat in the sink.

I stared at myself in the mirror, unable to recognize the person looking back. My reflection was a stranger — broken, hollow, silent. The uniform that once made me feel strong now felt like armor I didn't deserve to wear.

I wanted to scream, but nothing came out. Just the sound of the fluorescent light humming overhead, filling the room with a mechanical, indifferent buzz. I ran the tap and watched the water turn pink as it spiraled down the drain. It felt like everything inside me was draining with it.

For a long time, I stood there — one hand gripping the edge of the sink, the other pressed against my ribs — trying to steady my breathing, trying to remind myself that I was still alive. Every breath hurt, but each one proved that I hadn't disappeared.

Somewhere in the back of my mind, training kicked in: *Clean up. Get composed. Don't let anyone see.* The military teaches you how to survive everything except moments like this.

When I finally left the bathroom, the world outside looked exactly the same. My living room, the old futon with its sagging mattress, the noise of car traffic outside, the smell of my pasta, waiting for me on the stove — all unchanged. But I wasn't. Something in me had shifted, and I knew that nothing would ever be the same again.

That night, I learned how silence can be heavier than any weapon, and how survival doesn't always look brave — sometimes it just looks like standing, breathing, and pretending you're fine when every part of you isn't.

The days that followed felt like moving through fog. I couldn't hold onto thoughts for long; conversations slipped away as quickly as they came. It was as if my mind had decided that remembering too much would be fatal. I would start a sentence and forget where it was going, stare at an object without understanding why I was holding it. My short-term memory fractured, leaving me stranded in a haze of confusion and exhaustion.

Physically, my body carried the proof of what had happened, even when

I tried to deny it. My ribs ached when I breathed too deeply, my head throbbed constantly, and even the weight of a blanket felt unbearable some nights. Every movement reminded me of the violence I was trying so hard not to acknowledge. I learned quickly that pain could live quietly inside you, waiting for the smallest moment to make itself known.

Sleep became a battlefield. When I did close my eyes, I saw flashes—his face, the sound of the door, the feeling of being trapped. Nightmares blurred into waking life until I wasn't sure which was worse. I began to dread the darkness, pouring another drink just to quiet my mind long enough to get a few hours of escape. Drinking became routine, then necessity. It dulled the pain, blurred the edges, made it easier not to feel anything at all.

I stopped answering calls. I didn't tell my parents. I told myself it was to protect them, but the truth was simpler: I couldn't bear to say it out loud. To speak the words would make it real, and I wasn't ready for that kind of truth. So I stayed silent, smiling when I had to, pretending I was fine when I wasn't even close.

I became hypervigilant, constantly scanning my surroundings. Every sound felt like a threat, every shadow too close. My shoulders ached from the tension I carried there. I couldn't stand people walking behind me, couldn't tolerate loud voices, couldn't find comfort anywhere. The world had suddenly become dangerous, and I no longer trusted it—or anyone in it.

My personality began to shift in ways I didn't recognize. I used to be lighthearted, quick to laugh, eager to connect. Now I was guarded, sharp-edged, and withdrawn. I spoke less, felt less, and lived in a kind of emotional grayscale. Friends noticed the change, but no one pressed hard enough to break through the wall I had built around myself.

Inside, I was unraveling—quietly, invisibly. My body hurt, my mind raced, and my spirit dimmed. I told myself that if I could just make it through one more day, one more night, one more sunrise, maybe I'd start to feel human again.

But healing doesn't begin in silence. And back then, silence was all I had.

Chapter 4

The morning after the assault, I did what I was trained to do — I reported for duty.

Every step felt mechanical, my body moving through the motions while my mind hovered somewhere far above it all. My uniform was pressed, my hair pulled back, my face expressionless. On the outside, I looked just like every other any other soldier who had gotten into a scrape the night before, sporting my fat lip and swollen eye. Inside, I was shattered glass held together by willpower.

I didn't tell anyone. Not yet. How could I? The fear was louder than any words I could have formed. Fear of not being believed. Fear of being blamed. Fear that somehow, in some twisted way, it would come back on me.

My unit hallways were full of laughter that morning — music playing, people joking, voices echoing down the hall. It all sounded wrong, like the world had forgotten to stop and notice that mine had fallen apart.

When I passed him in the corridor a few days later, he didn't even look my way. Just walked past, laughing with a group of guys like nothing had ever happened. That moment almost broke me more than the assault itself. His ease, his freedom, the way the world moved around him untouched — it made me feel invisible.

I wanted to disappear, but instead, I did the only thing I knew how to do: I followed orders. I showed up. I pushed through.

Because in the military, pain doesn't grant you time off. And in that silence, I learned to wear my uniform like a disguise — one that hid my bruises, my fear, and my shame.

The weeks bled together, each day extinguished by the next. With every glass, the alcohol burned away the skeletal memory of the assault, leaving a fragile, narcotic peace. I found an anchor in town: Joshua. He was wonderfully peaceful, a man untouched by the life that had marred me. He still believed in true love and soul mates. He never locked his door before bed, never lay awake in the dark, tense and ready for a break-in.

I remember the two of us on a snowy evening, ordering Wendy's and driving my little Ford Focus through the untouched snow back to my apartment. The roads were quiet, the world soft and blanketed in white. I remember smiling—laughing, even—though it felt like my face might crack from the unfamiliar effort. It had been weeks since laughter had felt natural.

We ran inside, dodging icy patches, shedding the cold, and turned on *Bob's Burgers*. The room filled with the warmth of its absurd humor, and for the first time in a long while, I could feel my nerves begin to unclench. We traded stories about terrible first dates, our laughter bouncing off the walls of my tiny apartment until my stomach hurt from it.

Then, somehow, I started telling him about Seth—about that night. The words spilled out before I could stop them. My bones seemed to remember the pain all at once; the laughter died in my throat.

Silence.

More silence.

And then Joshua spoke, his voice breaking just enough to fracture my heart.

"That was rape. Stefanie, you were raped."

My throat went dry. The air felt heavy and sharp. In an instant, our lighthearted conversation turned to what came next—how to report, who to talk to, what the safest path forward might be. Joshua's eyes were soft but unwavering, his concern steady and real.

I remember wanting to collapse, to cry until my chest gave out. I didn't know then that this moment—this single, fragile night—would replay in my mind for years. I would turn it over again and again, searching for the point where everything shifted, where laughter became reckoning.

The day I finally decided to report the assault was filled with panic, anxiety, and an all-consuming sense of shame. I remember standing in formation, back straight, arms locked behind me, the sun beating down as sweat slid down my sides. My body was rigid, but inside, I was trembling.

Joshua's words kept echoing in my head: *"That was rape, Stefanie."*

Every time the phrase repeated, my stomach turned. Reporting meant saying it out loud. It meant admitting that it had happened—that I hadn't been able to stop it. That in the fight-or-flight moment, I'd fought, and still lost. Somewhere deep down, I carried the guilt that it was my fault.

I knew what happened to soldiers who reported sexual harassment, let alone assault. The whispered stories spread like wildfire—retaliation, alienation, ruined careers. I wanted to be Sergeant Marvin. I wanted to be the soldier who made her family proud. And I knew that this single decision could destroy all of that.

When formation finally broke, I spotted Sergeant Griest—someone I trusted, someone who always managed to make me laugh. My boots felt impossibly heavy as I walked toward him, the ground beneath me like wet concrete. He greeted me with a smile and a joke, but this time, I couldn't return it. The weight of what I was about to say pressed too hard on my chest.

I asked him to come into my office. Once the door shut, the words tumbled out before I could stop them. I told him everything. My voice shook at first, then steadied as I slipped into a kind of emotional autopilot. I described what happened as if I were reading a report about someone else—someone I barely knew.

When I finished, silence filled the room. The easy grin he always wore was gone. His voice was calm, but careful, when he finally spoke.

"Stefanie," he said, "I need to tell you—I'm the Sexual Harassment/Assault Response Coordinator for the unit."

Shit.

My heart dropped, but he stayed steady. He explained my options: I could walk away and nothing would move forward, or I could file a report. Then he said something I'll never forget.

"Whatever you decide to do, I'll be here for you."

I asked for time—just until the end of the day—to decide. He nodded. "Of course."

The hours crawled by. I tried to lose myself in my work, but my hands wouldn't stop fidgeting. I tapped my fingers on the desk, chewed at my nails, stared at the clock until the numbers blurred. Each passing minute felt like a countdown.

Finally, the end of the day came.

In or out. Report or don't report.

I left my office, scanning the hallway until I saw him standing with a group of soldiers, laughing about something small and ordinary. When he met my eyes, I just gave a small nod. He understood immediately.

Back in my office, I turned to him and said the words that changed everything:

"I want to report the assault."

The moment I said, *"I want to report the assault,"* the air in the room changed. It felt heavier—thicker somehow. Sergeant Griest nodded once, quiet and deliberate, and I could see the weight of what I'd just done reflected in his eyes.

There was no taking it back now.

He walked me through the next steps—forms, statements, official language that stripped my story down into bullet points and dates. Everything I said became evidence. Every detail, no matter how personal, was recorded in black ink on government paper.

I remember sitting there, pen trembling in my hand, as the words blurred in front of me. *Victim. Perpetrator. Incident.* None of it felt human. None of it sounded like me.

I answered question after question, my voice flat and distant, as if I were somewhere else entirely. I could feel the pain in my ribs again, dull but insistent. The lights in the office buzzed overhead, and the sound grated against my nerves. I just wanted to be invisible.

When it was done, I felt drained—like I'd run a marathon I never signed up for. Sergeant Griest thanked me for trusting him, but all I could manage was a weak nod. The truth was, I didn't feel brave. I felt exposed. Vulnerable. Raw.

Word spread quickly, as it always does. The sideways glances started within days. Conversations stopped when I entered a room. Some people avoided me completely; others were overly kind, like they were trying to prove something. The isolation was worse than I expected—it wrapped around me like cold air, reminding me constantly that I had broken an unspoken rule.

The nights became harder. Every sound jolted me awake. Every nightmare dragged me back into that room, that night. I started drinking more, telling myself it was just to take the edge off. But the truth was, I couldn't stop my mind from replaying everything—every moment, every choice, every what-if.

I tried to keep up appearances, to be the soldier I once was. But I wasn't the same. My focus slipped. My patience ran thin. I stopped laughing at jokes. I went through the motions each day, but my body was in survival mode—hyperaware, tense, waiting for something else to happen.

I remember walking past my reflection one morning and not recognizing myself. My eyes looked hollow, older somehow. There was a hardness in them that hadn't been there before.

Reporting didn't bring me peace. It brought clarity, maybe—but not peace. Still, part of me knew it was the first real step toward reclaiming something I'd lost. My voice. My truth.

Even if no one believed me, even if it cost me everything I'd worked for, at least I had said it out loud.

At least the silence was broken.

In the weeks that followed my report, everything around me shifted—quietly at first, then all at once.

The same people who used to joke with me at morning formation now avoided eye contact. Conversations died mid-sentence when I walked into a room. I could feel it—the discomfort, the curiosity, the judgment. I was no longer "Marvin" or "Sergeant-to-be." I was *that girl*.
    The one who reported. The one who said the word no one wanted to hear.

The silence was suffocating.

At first, I tried to convince myself that I was imagining it. That the sideways glances weren't really there, that the laughter behind closed doors wasn't about me. But deep down, I knew better. The military teaches you to read a room—to sense danger before it strikes. And this time, the danger wasn't physical. It was social. It was the quiet kind that isolates you until you start doubting your own reality.

My chain of command said all the right things—*We take this seriously. We support you.* But behind those words were pauses, paperwork delays, and meetings that made my stomach twist. Every "follow-up" felt like another interrogation. Every form, another reminder that my trauma had been reduced to case numbers and protocol.

The man who hurt me still walked freely around base. Sometimes I saw him in passing, his uniform crisp and unbothered. Each time, my breath caught in my throat, my body going rigid before I could stop it. I'd turn the other way, pretend I didn't see, but the image burned into me long after he was gone.

I started sleeping less. The nightmares came harder, sharper. I'd wake up drenched in sweat, my heart racing as if I were back there again. I drank more just to dull the edges, to find a few hours of numbness. The alcohol helped me get through the nights, but it made the days blur together. I was unraveling slowly, one sip at a time.

Work became unbearable. Tasks that used to take me minutes stretched into hours. My concentration was shot, my hands always trembling, my patience with people nearly gone. I avoided social gatherings, skipped meals, and disappeared into myself.

No one told me I was being punished, but I felt it in the way opportunities slipped away. I wasn't chosen for projects I once would've led. My evaluations grew colder, more clinical. It was as if speaking the truth had stripped me of my identity as a soldier.

Still, I kept showing up. Every morning, I put on my uniform and stood in formation, pretending not to notice the whispers or the space people left between us. Some part of me refused to let them win—to let the system's indifference erase who I was before that night.

There were moments when I questioned whether I should've stayed silent. Whether the peace of ignorance would've been better than this lonely kind of courage. But then I'd remember the words Joshua said, the ones that started it all: *"That was rape, Stefanie."*

And I knew I couldn't go back to silence.

Even when my voice trembled, even when no one wanted to hear it, it was mine. And I was going to keep using it.

Chapter 5

In the months after the assault, Joshua and I grew closer than ever. Eventually, we packed up my mismatched, thrifted belongings and moved them into his apartment. It felt like shedding an old skin—one that had seen too much.

Not long after, we got a dog—a tiny, runt-of-the-litter Great Pyrenees puppy we named Willow. She was all fluff and clumsy paws, a small creature who didn't yet know how big she'd someday be. Somehow, she made the world feel softer again.

That summer, in August 2016, Joshua took me to an art district in a nearby city. The air was thick and heavy, the kind of heat that clings to your skin, but I didn't care. The entire evening, I could barely contain the bubbling thought that looped in my head: *He's going to propose. He's going to propose.*

And he did.

Under strings of lights and fading twilight, he got down on one knee. For the first time in a long time, I felt like the world might just hold good things for me again.

Joshua was my anchor through everything that followed. He never asked me to relive the details. He sat beside me at every official interview and hearing, his quiet presence saying everything words could not. He was my lifeline.

Then one evening, as I stood in our tiny kitchen making dinner, with Willow napping just outside the doorway, everything changed with a single phone call.

The kitchen felt impossibly small—walls closing in, the air thick. I remember my hands gripping the too-short countertops, knuckles gone white, my phone lying on the cutting board beside the half-chopped vegetables. I could hear my own breathing—ragged, uneven—as though I'd just run miles uphill. My ribs ached with every inhale.

Then the call ended. Just like that.

The voice on the other end had spoken a sentence that didn't make sense, a jumble of words that my mind refused to understand.

"...unable to prosecute... so sorry."

It had been a year and a half since I reported. A year and a half of waiting, hoping, fighting to be heard. And now—nothing. No justice. No closure. Just those words.

My chest constricted. My vision narrowed. The room began to spin, and I clung to the counter to stay upright. My chef's knife lay beside the phone—beautiful, cared for, sharpened by my own hand. I stared at it, frozen.

Then, instead, I grabbed the nearest glass and hurled it at the wall. The sound shattered the silence, and Joshua came running.

All he saw was me collapsing—knees buckling, shoulders shaking, eyes wild and unfocused. My hands were throbbing from how tightly I'd gripped the counter, still desperate to hold onto *something*.

I sank to the floor. One hand clutched at my shirt, dragging the fabric over my mouth to muffle the sounds coming out of me—low, guttural, uncontrollable. The sobs came first, deep and convulsive. Then the screams followed.

They tore out of me before I could stop them—raw, animal sounds I didn't know I was capable of making. A wounded creature mourning not just what had happened, but the loss of any illusion that justice could heal it.

I didn't care if the neighbors heard. I didn't care if Joshua couldn't make sense of the words I wasn't saying. I just howled—grieving, broken, unashamed.

Because in that moment, there was nothing left to hold together.

After that night, everything went quiet. Not just around me—but inside me.

The screams had wrung me dry. What was left was hollow silence, heavy and endless. The kind that hums in your bones and makes every sound—every heartbeat—feel too loud.

Days blurred together. I woke up, went to work, came home, drank, slept, repeated. Existing felt like walking through wet cement, each movement heavy and deliberate. Joshua tried to help—he cooked, cleaned, held me when the nightmares came—but I had retreated somewhere he couldn't follow.

I was still breathing, but I wasn't living.

The military didn't offer closure, only paperwork. There were no apologies, no justice, no acknowledgment that something irreversible had happened. I was told to "move forward," as if grief were something you could clock out from at the end of the day.

But trauma doesn't follow orders.

For months, I carried the weight of that phone call in my chest like a stone. Every step hurt. Every breath reminded me that I was still here when, some nights, I didn't want to be.

And then came Willow.

She had grown from a clumsy puppy into a gentle, steady presence— always watching, always listening. On the worst days, when I couldn't get out of bed, she'd nudge her nose under my hand until I moved. When my body shook from panic, she'd press her weight against me, grounding me back in the present.

It was Willow who became the first real reason to keep trying. To get up, to go outside, to take one small step toward something that looked like life again.

At first, "healing" didn't look like progress. It looked like sitting in silence on the floor beside her. It looked like crying until I couldn't anymore. It looked like showing up to therapy, saying nothing, and coming back the next week anyway.

But little by little, the silence started to change. It softened. I began to speak—to Joshua, to my therapist, sometimes even to myself. Words I'd buried for years began to surface. Not all at once, but in fragments.

There were still nights when I felt the same grief rise in my chest—the same animalistic howl that had once torn through my kitchen. But now, instead of swallowing it, I let it exist. I learned that healing isn't about forgetting; it's about making space for the pain without letting it consume you.

I started to run again. I took Willow on long walks through quiet trails, feeling the wind, the rhythm of my breath, the steady click of her paws beside me. For the first time since that night, I felt something that almost resembled peace.

Joshua never stopped showing up. Even when I couldn't meet his eyes, even when I pulled away, he stayed. And though I didn't know it then, the version of me who clawed her way back from that floor—the woman who chose to keep living—was beginning to take shape.

Healing wasn't a single moment of triumph. It was thousands of tiny choices to stay.

To stand up.
  To breathe.
  To begin again.

Chapter 6

For a little while, I thought I was finally okay.

After everything, after the first assault, after the months of feeling like I was walking through fire, Joshua's proposal felt like air. He knelt down under the yellow glow of the streetlights in that art district — sweat glistening on his forehead, his hands trembling just a little. My heart was pounding so hard I could barely hear the words. When he asked, I said yes before he even finished the question.

For the first time in so long, I felt chosen for something good.

I moved my thrifted furniture, my threadbare clothes, my whole small life, into his apartment. We had our growing puppy, Willow — this tiny Great Pyrenees runt who couldn't climb the stairs without falling on her face. She was soft, silly, bursting with joy and chaos, and I thought, *This is what healing looks like.* Joshua made me breakfast. We made plans. I let myself believe that maybe the worst parts of me had already happened.

But healing doesn't always ask your permission. It doesn't move in a straight line. Sometimes it snaps.

The day everything broke again, the air on base was heavy — a quiet that didn't feel peaceful. Eyes followed me. Whispers grew louder than footsteps. I knew something was wrong before it happened.

Before they made sure I'd pay for speaking up.

At the final formation of the day, my name was barked by our platoon sergeant. "MARVIN, be in the conference room after final formation."

I had no idea why I was being summoned after everyone left for the day. As I walked into the conference room, I saw that there were only three sergeants sitting in there.

My platoon sergeant, my squad leader, and my team leader.

Fuck-I thought.

The noise of the day ending quickly receded in the building hallways, as everyone scrambled to leave to go home for the day, yet I willingly sat down at the conference table without a word.

"I'm pissed," said my platoon sergeant.

"I'm pissed because I'm hearing slander about a good soldier. Slander that, in my opinion, could ruin an entire career, based on an UN-FOUNDED accusation."

My hands gripped the wooden conference table, gripping into the edge. My white knuckles shone through my skin from gripping so hard. My platoon sergeant continued, despite the tears of fear pricking my eyes.

"How in the HELL can you be so selfish and ridiculously stupid for doing that to another soldier??"

"Get up."

Confused, but with a deep fear of what was happening next, I rose from my chair. The back of my legs were slick with sweat.

CRACK.

A fist made contact with my cheekbone, my eye felt like it was going to explode. The blow knocked my off of my feet, with me barely catching myself from falling by grabbing the table on my way down.

I looked up to see my squad leader move in front of the door, blocking the window from view.

Double Fuck-I thought.

Hands grabbed at my body, everywhere and all at once. My hair was pulled out of it's slicked back bun.

There are moments you don't remember in pictures but in sensations. Cold linoleum. The smell of sweat and metal. The feeling of your own body betraying you. The shock, then the numbness, then the pain that doesn't live in the skin but in the soul.

When all three of them were done, I was pulled back onto my feet and pulled into my office. I barely remember what happened next, getting dressed, or getting into my car and driving home, but I made it.

When I finally made it home, I remember staring at the wall for a long time, tracing cracks in the paint with my eyes, because moving meant acknowledging what had happened again — that it happened *again*. My hands were shaking. My heartbeat was a dull thud, slow and distant. My whole body was loud, but my voice was gone.

The days after were worse.

The people I had trained with, eaten with, laughed with — they looked right through me. Some smirked when I passed. Some whispered things I can still hear, sharp and deliberate. I'd walk into a room and the air would shift, and I'd know the story had spread, twisted, used against me.

I wasn't a survivor anymore. I was a problem.

They said I was asking for attention. That I was ruining good men's careers. That I was lucky it wasn't worse.

I stopped sleeping. I stopped eating. I started walking everywhere with my keys in my hand like a weapon.

Joshua, who had no idea what had happened, held me at night, his thumb tracing my spine, wanting love, as any fiancee would. But I could feel the distance in me — the quiet hollow where my laughter used to be. I'd look at Willow asleep at our feet and think, *She has no idea how broken her person is.*

I tried to tell myself I'd survived worse. That surviving once meant I could do it again.

But the second time wasn't just an assault — it was the betrayal of everything I'd believed the uniform stood for.

And yet, even in the quiet, I could still feel the pulse of something deep inside me — small, defiant, steady. A whisper that said: *You are still here. You are still here*

The days that followed blurred together — a haze of paperwork, cold stares, and whispered words that stung worse than the bruises. The same people who once stood beside me now turned their backs. Some of them smirked when they passed me in the halls. Others just looked through me like I wasn't there.

There's a kind of loneliness that comes after being hurt like that — not the kind that comes from being alone, but from being unseen. I walked through each day pretending I didn't hear, didn't notice, didn't feel. But every word, every look, every laugh carved deeper into me.

At night, I'd crawl into bed beside Joshua and lie perfectly still, pretending to be asleep long before he came into the room. I didn't know how to tell him what had happened. I didn't want to see the look in his eyes — that mixture of love and helplessness that made me feel even smaller.

Willow was still a puppy then, all legs and heart, tripping over both. She'd curl up at the edge of the bed, pressing her warm little body against my feet. Sometimes she'd lift her head in the dark, ears twitching, like she could hear the things I couldn't say.

One night, Joshua reached for my hand. I flinched before I could stop myself. The hurt on his face was immediate, and it broke me in ways the others never could. I turned toward the wall and whispered, "I'm sorry."

He said, "You don't have to be sorry." But we both knew I was — for surviving, for shutting down, for not being the same girl he'd proposed to.

Our wedding came a few months later.

It was a hot, cloudless July day — the kind of day people call perfect. My skirt and top were simple, blush pink satin that caught the sunlight just enough to look alive, with a simple white, sleeveless top, and jeweled belt.

Joshua looked nervous and happy all at once, standing at the end of that short aisle like he couldn't believe I was really walking toward him. The air smelled liked wildflowers and pine. Somewhere in the distance, a car alarm chirped, then stopped — the kind of noise that shouldn't mean anything, but made my heart race anyway.

People smiled at me. Cameras flashed. The judge said words I barely heard. Every time Joshua reached for my hand, I fought the urge to pull away. His fingers were warm, steady, good — but my body didn't know the difference between love and danger anymore. My brain kept flickering like a broken light: *you're safe — you're not. You're loved — you're trapped.*

When he said, "I do," I wanted to feel that joy, that sense of arrival. Instead, I felt a hollow ache where the joy should've been. I smiled for the pictures, tilted my chin just right, pretended I wasn't shaking inside. When he kissed me, I felt the whole crowd exhale, waiting for a love story they could believe in. I gave them one. I gave myself one, too —

or tried to.

That night, after everyone was gone, I sat on the edge of our bed, staring at the bouquet on the nightstand. My hands were trembling, not from excitement, but from the weight of everything that had led me there — the bruises that had faded, the memories that hadn't. Joshua touched my shoulder gently, and my whole body flinched before I could stop it. He froze. I saw the confusion, the hurt, the guilt. And all I could whisper was, "I'm sorry."

He didn't ask for an explanation. He just sat beside me, took my hand, and said, "You don't have to be sorry. We'll figure this out."

But I could see it — the way my pain hovered between us, unspoken but present, like a guest who never left.

Later, people would say our wedding was beautiful. That I glowed. That we looked so in love. I wanted to believe them. But when I look back at the photos, I can see it now — the tightness in my smile, the way my eyes seem to look past the lens, searching for something I couldn't name yet.

It wasn't that I didn't love him. I did, immensely. It's that trauma had moved into the same house we did, quietly unpacking its boxes, settling into the corners of our new life.

Joshua didn't know what was wrong, whether it was aftermath and fallout from the first assault, or something else. He didn't know the trainwreck that was my head.

There were mornings I couldn't look at the rings on my finger. It gleamed too bright against the gray of everything else. I'd twist it around and around, wondering if I'd ever feel like the woman who'd once worn it proudly, who'd said 'I do' because she believed she still had a future.

I started going through the motions again — shower, uniform, work, silence. My body moved, but my mind stayed trapped in that night. The military's investigation went nowhere. I learned that "reporting" didn't mean "believed." It meant branded. I didn't even bother reporting the second assault, or telling anyone in my life until years later.

Still, Joshua stayed. He waited out my bad days, my long silences. When I couldn't talk, he'd just sit beside me, his hand resting palm-up between us, patient. Sometimes, when I was brave enough, I'd place my hand in his. The warmth would startle me every time — proof that I was still here, still capable of feeling something that wasn't fear.

It was Willow who saved me, in small ways at first. She'd nudge my hand when I drifted too far away. She'd insist on walks, even when I wanted to hide from the world. She didn't care that I was broken — she just wanted to be near me.

There was one afternoon when it all cracked open. I was sitting on the floor, surrounded by laundry I couldn't bring myself to fold, when she crawled into my lap and laid her head on my chest. Her heartbeat thumped against mine, steady and real. I started to cry — the kind of cry that comes from somewhere deeper than words — and for the first time, I didn't stop it. I let it come.

That was the moment I realized healing wouldn't be some sudden, beautiful thing. It would be a long, uneven road made of tiny moments

— of warmth, of trust, of relearning how to exist in a world that had taken so much.

Eventually, I'd find Leland — the dog who would change everything, who would become my constant, my anchor. But before Leland, there was this: Joshua's quiet presence. Willow's unwavering love. My own slow, painful decision to keep breathing, to keep moving, to keep choosing life.

Because even in the ruins, there was still something left — a small, stubborn spark that refused to go out. And that, I realized, was where healing began.

Chapter 7

By the spring of 2018, I was surviving — not living, just enduring one day at a time. The world had quieted into something dull and colorless. I got up, went to work, came home, took Willow for a walk, and tried not to think. The sharp edges of grief had worn down, but the ache remained — steady, familiar, always there.

Sometimes I'd catch myself staring out a window or into the mirror and wonder if this was it. If survival was all I was meant for now.

Willow was still my constant shadow, patient and loyal. She had carried me through nights when I could barely breathe, through days when I didn't speak to anyone at all. But as the panic attacks grew sharper and the nightmares clawed their way back with new ferocity, I began to realize I needed more than comfort. I needed a way to *live* again—not just survive the aftermath.

That's when I found Sierra Delta and Dogs Inc.

By that point, I had been rejected from eleven different service dog programs across the country. Each one said the same thing: my PTSD wasn't from combat—it was from military sexual trauma. And that, somehow, made me ineligible.

After what felt like the thousandth rejection call, the woman on the other end of the line paused before hanging up. "Hold on," she said quietly. "I have a number for a Marine who might be able to help you—but you didn't get it from me, understand?"

I promised I understood, scribbled the number down with shaking hands, and called immediately.

"Hello, you've reached BJ Ganem. How can I help you?"

Within a week, I was on a forty-five-minute phone call with BJ and his business partner, Mick Gillitzer. I told them my story in the only way I knew how—brisk, clinical, detached.

But nothing could have prepared me for what came next.

"Stefanie," BJ said gently, "thank you for sharing your story with us. Let's get you a service dog. But—you'll need to do some legwork and fill out applications."

Tears welled in my eyes before I could stop them. It was the first time anyone had said *yes*.

Mick mentioned an organization in Florida— Dogs Inc—and my fingers flew to the keyboard faster than they ever had before. For the first time in a long time, I felt something, so small, spark inside me again.

Hope.

The mission of Dogs Inc caught me immediately: pairing service dogs with veterans to help them rebuild their lives. The words *rebuild* and *freedom* leapt off the page. It had been so long since either of those had felt possible.

Applying wasn't easy. It meant opening old wounds, explaining in detail the things I had tried so hard not to relive — the fear, the triggers, the nights I woke up gasping for air. But for once, I wasn't treated like a problem to be fixed. The people at Dogs Inc didn't look away when I spoke. They didn't rush me or question the legitimacy of my trauma. They listened. They believed me.

Only a month before that, I had received my honorable discharge from the military — a phrase that sounded so clean and dignified on paper, but carried the weight of everything that had broken me. I had served with pride once, convinced that uniform meant belonging, purpose, redemption. But after the assault, everything changed. My body stayed, but my spirit had already begun to leave. Each day felt like survival training of a different kind — not of endurance, but of silence.

When the paperwork finally came through, it was bittersweet. "Honorable" meant I had done my duty. "Discharge" meant I was no longer welcome in the place that had once defined me. It meant the military had decided I was too damaged to continue — that my PTSD, born from the very environment meant to protect me, made me unfit to serve.

I remember standing in my living room holding that envelope, my hands trembling as if the paper itself carried the memories I tried so hard to bury. There was relief, yes, but also grief — the kind that doesn't have a name. I had survived, but I had lost the version of myself who believed in the system, in the promise of service and honor.

So when I applied for a service dog, I wasn't just filling out forms. I was searching for something to hold onto, something to rebuild from. It took months of paperwork, interviews, and waiting. I told myself not to get my hopes up, but a small, fragile part of me did anyway.

And then, one warm April afternoon, I got the call — exactly one month after my honorable discharge. For the first time in what felt like years, I felt the faint flicker of something I'd thought was gone for good — excitement.

Dogs Inc had found my match.

I'll never forget the first time I met him. The air hung heavy with summer heat, the kind that clings to your skin before you've even stepped out of the car. By the time I walked onto the Dogs Inc campus, sweat was already soaking through my shirt. The trainers gathered all of us—prospective service dog recipients—into the dormitory common room to announce our matches. I found a chair in the corner, surrounded by fellow veterans. For the first time in a long time, I felt like I could breathe. My shoulders dropped. My fingers stilled. I was among people who understood without needing to say a word.

Each dog at Dogs Inc carries a name chosen by a donor—sometimes to honor a loved one, sometimes to commemorate a story. Katie, one of the trainers, began reading off the pairings, describing each dog in tender, affectionate detail, sharing the meaning behind their names. With every name she called, my heart thudded harder, the wait stretching unbearably.

Finally, her gaze landed on me.

"Stefanie," she said, smiling, "your dog's name is Leland."

She paused. "He's a yellow Lab—almost white—and bigger than most of the dogs in this class. Are you sure you're okay with that?"

There wasn't a shred of hesitation. "Yes," I said, breathless.

Then came the moment we'd all been waiting for.

We were told to wait in our dorm rooms, leash in hand, until our dogs arrived. I sat at the small desk, my knee bouncing uncontrollably. The leather leash felt slick in my sweaty palms. Every second crawled.

Then—*a knock.*

One of the trainers peeked through the doorway. "Are you ready to meet your dog?!"

All I could do was nod.

BOOM.

The door burst open, and in bounded a gorgeous yellow Lab, barreling toward me with joyful abandon. He hit me square in the chest, knocking me clean out of the chair. Suddenly, I was on the floor, laughing through tears, as seventy-five pounds of pure joy covered my face in kisses, his tail thudding against every surface in the room like a drumbeat.

"Leland, sit!" the trainer instructed.

He obeyed instantly, tail still wagging, tongue hanging from a wide, happy mouth. She handed me the leash, and I clipped it onto his collar. The moment the buckle clicked into place, something inside me shifted—something I hadn't felt in years.

Peace.

When I finally sat back down, I took him in fully—a golden-coated, steady-eyed companion sitting perfectly still, waiting for my cue. His gaze met mine, calm and curious, as if he were studying the pieces of me that life had scattered.

I knelt down, and the wild energy that had filled the room moments before melted away. Without hesitation, Leland leaned forward and rested his head against my leg. Just like that. No testing, no uncertainty. As if he already knew.

The world seemed to pause. The endless static in my head faded to quiet. For the first time in so long, I felt peace.

Over the next few weeks, we trained together every day. The trainers at Dogs, Inc worked with us to build trust, teaching me how to read Leland's cues and teaching him how to respond to mine. It was exhausting and humbling — two steps forward, one step back.

There were moments I doubted myself. Trauma had made me wary of relying on anyone or anything, even a dog whose only goal was to help me. But Leland didn't care how broken I felt. He didn't need explanations. When my breathing quickened, he nudged me. When I froze, he leaned his weight against me until I remembered that I was still here. He was teaching me presence — to feel without drowning in it.

He also made me laugh again. Real, unguarded laughter. The kind that startled me the first few times it escaped. He had a way of looking at me when I was overthinking something — tilting his head, almost exasperated, as if to say, *"You're safe. Breathe."*

When I finally brought him home, Willow greeted him with cautious curiosity. Within days, they became inseparable — the old soul and the new guardian. Watching them together filled me with a kind of peace I hadn't felt since before the assault.

Leland quickly became more than a service dog. He became my lifeline — a living, breathing reminder that healing doesn't mean forgetting. It means learning how to move forward with the memories, not in spite of them.

With him by my side, I started doing things I hadn't done in years. I went to crowded stores without feeling like every exit was a trap. I took walks alone again. I went out for coffee. Simple things that most people take for granted, but for me, they were victories. Each one was proof that the world could still hold beauty, safety, and maybe even joy.

Sometimes, when we're walking together, I think about the woman I used to be — the one curled up on the kitchen floor, breaking apart. I wish I could tell her about this moment, about this calm golden dog trotting faithfully beside her. I'd tell her that peace doesn't always come from people or places — sometimes it comes on four paws, with eyes that see through the noise and say, *"You're safe now."*

Because of Leland, I learned that survival isn't the end of the story. It's the beginning.

Chapter 8

When I left Dogs Inc with Leland by my side, the world looked different. Not brighter exactly, but steadier—like the ground beneath me had finally stopped shifting. I was still carrying the weight of everything that had happened, but for the first time, I wasn't carrying it alone. Leland moved through the world with quiet confidence, anchoring me when the memories came, guiding me through moments that once felt impossible.

That summer, with his leash in my hand and hope flickering somewhere deep inside me, I made a decision that had once felt out of reach. I was going back to college.

Hope has a quiet way of returning—it doesn't shout or announce itself. It hums softly beneath your ribs until one day, you notice it again. That's how it felt leaving Dogs Inc with Leland. His steady footsteps matched mine, his calm presence reminding me that I was still here. Still capable of rebuilding.

With that same quiet courage, I took my next step toward healing. I enrolled back in the same college that I had almost failed out of years before.

Going back wasn't easy. Just filling out the application made my palms sweat, my heart racing with the old voices whispering that I'd fail again. The thought of crowded classrooms, fluorescent lights, and people brushing past me in the hallways made my stomach tighten. But every time I felt that fear rising, I'd glance down, and there he was—Leland—sitting patiently at my side, eyes soft and knowing.

The first day of class, I must have checked my backpack a dozen times before even stepping out the door. I packed everything twice—textbooks, pens, water bottle, Leland's collapsible bowl, treats, his vest—anything to keep my nerves occupied. As we walked across campus, I felt the weight of stares, curious eyes lingering on the big yellow Lab in his working vest. I tried to ignore them, focusing instead on the rhythmic click of his paws against the concrete.

It wasn't until I reached the classroom door that I realized I was holding my breath. Leland nudged my knee gently, grounding me back in the moment. I exhaled, gave the "forward" command, and we stepped inside together.

The room went quiet. The professor paused mid-sentence, a few students looked up from their laptops, and I could feel my face flush hot. But Leland didn't care. He moved with quiet confidence to the spot I pointed to beside my desk, circled twice, and settled down, his head resting gently on my shoe.

In that moment, I realized something important: I wasn't just going back to school. I was reclaiming the parts of myself I'd been too afraid to reach for. And I wasn't doing it alone anymore.

The days that followed were a fog of mental exhaustion and

adjustment—learning class schedules, finding quiet corners on campus, and figuring out how to navigate my new life with Leland by my side. Every building, every hallway, came with its own challenge: crowded stairwells, sudden noises, the tension that came with not knowing what was around the next corner. But where my anxiety once would have taken over, Leland was there. One gentle nudge from his nose, one weight of his head against my knee, and the chaos around me softened.

As the weeks went by, something remarkable happened. I began to open up—to people, to experiences, to the possibility that my story wasn't over.

A few months into the semester, I received an email from Greek Life inviting me to a sorority event. At first, I laughed it off; it felt like something that belonged to another lifetime, another version of me. But I looked down at Leland, with his golden eyes and eyebrows knit together, focusing on me, and eventually I said yes.

That night changed everything.

The women I met there didn't treat me like a project or a survivor—they treated me like a person. They asked about Leland, about my classes, about the books I liked to read. For the first time in years, I felt myself laughing freely, not the cautious kind that comes with watching your own reactions, but the kind that bubbles up before you can stop it.

When I accepted their bid, I didn't know what to expect. But my sorority became a kind of family—a circle of women who celebrated my small victories and showed up when life felt heavy. Leland quickly became their unofficial mascot, always stationed at my side during study sessions or philanthropy events, soaking up affection from anyone who passed by.

With their support, and with Leland's steady grounding, I found my rhythm. I joined an honor society, kept my GPA high, and even made the Dean's List. Each accomplishment, no matter how small, felt like reclaiming another piece of myself.

Even as I rebuilt the pieces of my life, life itself reminded me—healing is messy, uneven, and real.

Then, just as everything seemed to be falling into place, life shifted again.

I got the call about my dad on an ordinary afternoon—a day filled with classes, coffee, and plans for dinner with my sorority sisters. The world, once so bright and full of motion, came to a screeching halt. My dad was gone. Suddenly. No warning.

We hadn't spoken since my wedding in 2017. The silence between us had grown into something heavy and complicated, filled with hurt that neither of us had ever found the words to mend. When the news came, the guilt hit me like a wave. The finality of it all—the realization that there would be no chance for reconciliation—left me hollow.

That night, I sat on the floor of my apartment, still in my class clothes, phone screen dim beside me, and cried until I couldn't anymore. Leland stayed pressed against me the entire time, his head resting in my lap, his eyes soft and patient. He didn't move, didn't try to fix it—he just *stayed*. And somehow, that was enough.

Grief has a way of rearranging everything. For weeks, I went through the motions, attending classes, showing up for group meetings, smiling when people smiled at me. But inside, I felt raw and untethered. Still, every morning, Leland would nudge me out of bed, tail wagging, ready to face another day. And slowly, I did too.

It took time, but I found a strange kind of peace in knowing that my dad's story, like mine, was messy and unfinished—and that forgiveness, even unspoken, can still exist in the quiet spaces between loss and love.

Looking back, I realize that college was never just about finishing what I'd started—it was about learning how to live again. Every exam I passed, every late-night study session, every walk across campus with Leland at my side was proof that I could still move forward, even with the past clinging to me. Healing didn't come all at once, or in grand moments of triumph. It came in small, steady ways—in laughter shared with my sorority sisters, in the warmth of friendship that expected nothing from me, in the rhythm of Leland's paws on the pavement when everything else felt uncertain.

I came to understand that survival isn't the same as living. For a long time, I'd only been surviving—breathing, existing, but not really *being*. It took time, patience, and a lot of tears, but I started to see that my life wasn't defined by what had been taken from me, but by what I was still capable of building.

Grief and growth wove themselves together like threads of the same story—one teaching me to let go, the other teaching me to begin again. And through it all, Leland remained my constant—my anchor when the world felt too heavy, my reminder that love could still be pure and steady.

Time has a way of softening even the sharpest edges of grief. The years that followed were full of small victories—some loud, others quiet—but each one a step further from the girl who once believed her life had already been written for her.

When graduation day finally came, I felt that familiar rush of nerves—the same kind I'd felt at Dogs Inc, the same I'd felt on my first day back in class. But this time, it wasn't fear. It was gratitude.

Leland and I both wore caps and gowns that day. His, specially made by one of my sorority sisters, matched mine perfectly—tiny tassel and all. Across my cap, I had carefully written, *"I hope my dog is proud of me."* Across his, in bold letters, it read, *"I am."*

As we waited in line to walk the stage, I looked down at him—my steadfast partner, my anchor, my quiet reminder that healing was possible. He looked back up at me, tail sweeping the floor, as if he knew exactly what this moment meant.

When they called our names—both of our names—the entire auditorium erupted in cheers. I could hear my sorority sisters screaming from the stands, see my professors smiling through tears, and feel the weight of everything I'd overcome pressing gently against my chest.

As we crossed the stage, side by side, I felt it again—the same quiet, steady thing I'd felt that very first day when I clipped his leash onto his collar.

Hope.

Because this wasn't just a graduation. It was proof that even after the worst chapters of your story, new ones can still be written—beautiful, unexpected, full of light.

And through it all, Leland was there. Not just as my service dog, but as the living reminder that love can guide you home.

Chapter 9

Life after graduation felt strangely still at first. For years, my days had been measured by class schedules, assignments, and late-night study sessions with Leland's head resting on my knee. Now, the quiet was different—gentler, but uncertain. I found myself wondering, *What now?*

Leland adjusted easily. Wherever I went, he was there—steady, patient, grounding me in every new transition. He had walked beside me through fear and grief, and now he was walking with me into something completely new: peace.

Then came the moment that would change everything again.

When I found out I was pregnant, I sat on the edge of the bed, one hand resting on my stomach, the other in Leland's fur. I whispered, "You're going to be a big brother," and I swear, his tail thumped like he understood. Through morning sickness, exhaustion, and the tidal wave of emotions that pregnancy brought, Leland was always close. He'd nudge me out of bed when I couldn't find the energy, rest his chin on my belly when I cried, and later—when the baby started kicking—he'd tilt his head curiously, as if to say, *Who's in there?*

When James was born, everything shifted again. The moment we brought him home, Leland's whole demeanor softened. He'd stand guard by the bassinet, his tail sweeping slowly whenever James stirred. When Willow—the same spirited Great Pyrenees who had once inspired me to get Leland—joined in, the two of them became an unlikely team. Willow would hover protectively nearby, and Leland would curl close, calm and deliberate, as if teaching her the sacredness of stillness.

There were nights when I'd rock James to sleep, exhausted and unsure, the weight of new motherhood pressing on me. I'd look down and see both dogs at my feet—Leland watching me with quiet understanding, Willow with her head resting near James's tiny blanket. It felt like my little family was healing something deep and unseen, together.

Becoming a mother was a kind of rebirth for me, too. I began to see the world through softer eyes, not just as a survivor, but as someone who could create safety and love in the same world that had once hurt me. The strength I'd once used to simply survive became something else—a drive to help others do the same.

That's when the spark for advocacy began to grow. I started speaking more openly about my story—about military sexual trauma, about Leland's role in my healing, and about the power of service dogs to restore not just function, but *hope*. What began as quiet conversations turned into something larger: panel talks, veteran outreach, helping other survivors navigate their own paths toward peace.

Leland remained my silent partner through it all, sitting beside me at every event, every interview, every trembling first step into vulnerability. He'd rest his head on my foot while I spoke, his calm presence anchoring me to the moment. And every time I saw someone's eyes fill with recognition or relief, I knew why I had made it through everything I had—so I could help others believe that healing was possible, too.

My life no longer felt divided into *before* and *after*. It felt whole. Messy, imperfect, beautifully whole.

And at the center of it all—Leland, Willow, Joshua, and our baby boy—was the life I never thought I'd get to live.

Epilogue

Sometimes, when the house is finally still—when James is asleep, Willow is snoring softly by the door, and Leland is curled at my feet—I think about how far we've come.

There was a time when I didn't believe peace like this could exist. When the world felt too sharp, too loud, too broken to live in. But here I am, years later, surrounded by a kind of love I once thought was out of reach.

Healing doesn't look like what I thought it would. It's not the absence of pain. It's the presence of gentleness after the storm. It's a baby's laugh, a warm muzzle pressed against your hand, the feeling of your husband's arm around you when nightmares fade into morning light.

Leland has grown older now. His muzzle is silvering, his pace a little slower, but his eyes still hold that same calm steadiness that met me all those years ago in a tiny dorm room at Dogs Inc. He's been there for every chapter—the breaking, the rebuilding, the becoming. He taught me how to trust again, how to stay, how to believe in a future I couldn't yet see.

When I speak now—at veteran events, at survivor gatherings, or in quiet conversations with those who are still in the thick of their pain—I tell them this: healing isn't a finish line. It's a path you walk, one step at a time, often with trembling hands and tear-streaked faces. But if you're lucky, you'll have someone—or something—to walk it with you.

For me, that someone was a yellow Lab named Leland.

I used to think survival was the end of my story. Now I know—it was only the beginning. Because survival is what brought me here: to love, to motherhood, to advocacy, to the quiet peace of an ordinary night surrounded by the life I built from the ashes.

And as I sit here, with Leland breathing softly beside me and James dreaming down the hall, I finally understand what hope really is.

It's not loud or triumphant. It's quiet. Patient. Steady.

It's the space between heartbeats—the place where survival turns into living.

Photo taken by Stefanie during her mission in Chapter 3-January 2016

Photo taken the day of the first assault-January 2016

College Graduation Day-May 2022

Stefanie and Leland at the Nashville Soccer Club-October 2025

Stefanie (pregnant with James), Joshua, and Leland-October 2024

SALVO

Author's Note

To every survivor who finds their way to these pages—you are not alone. I see you. I believe you. I know how heavy it can feel to carry a story that no one else seems to understand. But I promise you this: your story does not end in pain. There is life waiting for you beyond the breaking. There is healing, laughter, love, and hope that will find its way back to you, even when you stop searching for it.

To those who walked beside me on my own journey—thank you for holding the light when I couldn't see it.

To Joshua, my anchor and best friend, who saw me not as what I'd survived, but as who I could become—thank you for choosing me every single day.

To James, my sweet son, you are proof that life after darkness can be filled with light. You are my reason, my reminder that healing isn't just about surviving—it's about growing something beautiful from the broken places.

To Willow, whose spirit started it all, and to Leland, who carried me through the hardest parts and stayed by my side through every new beginning—you are both woven into every heartbeat of this story.

To my family-my parents, for loving me through the silences, for the forgiveness and understanding that came when I needed it most.

To my little sister, Maddie—thank you for being a steady, loving presence in my life. Your kindness, patience, and quiet strength have grounded me through every storm. I am endlessly grateful for you.

To my sorority sisters, who reminded me how to laugh again, who turned ordinary days into moments of joy and belonging—thank you for loving Leland as much as you love me. To Sophie, to Mary, to Hailey, to Allie, to Lily, to Dawson, to Anna, to Erin...all of you hold a place in my heart.

And to every person reading this—may you find your version of hope.

May you know that healing is not linear, not perfect, but worth every step.

May you believe, even on the hardest days, that you are deserving of peace.

With love,
Stefanie Marvin-Miller and Leland

Made in the USA
Middletown, DE
04 December 2025

22379738R00050